SCHOLASTIC

Hi-Lo Passages
TO BUILD
Comprehension

Grades 7–8
by Michael Priestley

New York • Toronto • London • Auckland • Sydney
Mexico City • New Delhi • Hong Kong • Buenos Aires

Teaching *Resources*

Cover design by Maria Lilja
Interior design by Creative Pages, Inc.
Interior illustrations by Jennifer Emery, pages 26 & 27, 40; Eva Vagreti Cockrille, pages 11, 5 & 6; Drew-Brook-Cormack, pages 33, 44; Kate Flanagan, page 18; Ka Botzis, page 30; Kathleen Kemly, page 8; Holly Jones, pages 26 & 27.

ISBN: 0-439-54889-6

6 7 8 9 10   40   13 12 11 10

Hi-Lo Passages to Build Comprehension

Grades 7–8

Contents

		Readability
A Note for Teachers	4	Level
1. **Frog Fest** (Cause and Effect)	5	5.10
2. **On Being Yourself** (Author's Purpose and Point of View)	7	5.30
3. **Snip, Snip** (Sequence)	8	5.40
4. **On Top of the World** (Making Inferences and Predictions)	10	5.50
5. **The Dog for You** (Comparing and Contrasting)	12	5.60
6. **The Snowball** (Making Inferences and Predictions)	14	5.70
7. **River Raft Adventure!** (Fact and Opinion)	15	5.75
8. **Let Everyone Play!** (Author's Purpose and Point of View)	17	5.80
9. **School Uniforms? Think Again!** (Fact and Opinion)	19	5.85
10. **Meet a Snowboard Champ** (Drawing Conclusions)	21	5.90
11. **The Mysterious "Black Box"** (Cause and Effect)	23	5.95
12. **Ronnie's Restaurant Review** (Author's Purpose and Point of View)	25	5.95
13. **Making a Sled Kite** (Steps in a Process)	26	6.00
14. **It's a Wild and Wonderful Ride, But Is It Safe?** (Main Idea and Supporting Details)	28	6.00
15. **Isabel Leaves a Trail of Destruction** (Drawing Conclusions)	30	6.05
16. **Stick-to-it-ive Brian** (Story Elements)	31	6.10
17. **Blue Jeans** (Comparing and Contrasting)	33	6.30
18. **Welcome to Moviefans.com!** (Drawing Conclusions)	35	6.35
19. **Come Meet Our New Pals—The Sloth Bears** (Comparing and Contrasting)	37	6.40
20. **Spiders** (Fact and Opinion)	38	6.40
21. **Book Review—*Darkness Over Denmark: The Danish Resistance and the Rescue of the Jews*** (Cause and Effect)	39	6.45
22. **Egg Rolls** (Steps in a Process)	40	6.50
23. **Vote for Zach and . . .** (Story Elements)	41	6.60
24. **LeBron James Launches P.E. Program and a New Career** (Main Idea and Supporting Details)	43	6.85
25. **Evelyn Trout: A Remarkable Woman** (Main Idea and Supporting Details)	44	7.00
Answer Key	46	

A Note for Teachers

Reading is the key to learning, and today's students read materials from an ever-increasing number of sources. They must understand what they read in traditional forms of fiction and nonfiction, such as stories and textbooks. They must also comprehend newer forms of text, such as Web sites and e-mail on the Internet. Many students can benefit from more practice in reading, but finding good examples of hi-lo texts for instruction at the appropriate grade level can be challenging.

How to Use This Book

The main purpose of this book is to provide high-interest passages for students to read. All the passages in this book are intended to be motivating and interesting to seventh- and eighth-grade students, but they are written for readers one to two grade levels behind. You can find the readability score for each passage in the table of contents. (Passages were scored using the Dale-Chall scoring criteria and range in level of difficulty from 5.10 to 7.00.) These passages can be used for practice and instruction in reading and to help prepare students for taking tests. Most important, they can help students enjoy what they read.

This book provides 25 grade-appropriate passages in a wide variety of genres, including informational articles, letters, interviews, e-mail correspondence, and how-to guides. The passages target comprehension skills, such as making inferences or comparing and contrasting. Each passage has three or five comprehension questions based on skills. The questions are intended mainly to help students think about what they have read. (If you want to check students' responses, you may refer to the Answer Key at the back of the book.)

These questions will also help you assess students' comprehension of the material and allow students to practice answering test questions. There are multiple-choice and short-answer questions. Some of the passages include writing prompts to elicit longer responses.

Extending Activities

For some of these passages, you may want to have students go beyond answering the questions that are provided. For example, for any given passage you could have students write a summary of the selection in their own words or rewrite the passage from a different point of view. For some pairs of texts, you might have students compare and contrast the two selections. For other passages, you might want to create writing prompts and have students write full-length essays about what they have learned. Students will benefit from reading and analyzing these passages, discussing them in class or in small groups, and writing about them in a variety of ways.

Name _____ Date _____

Passage 1   Cause and Effect

Frog Fest

Gwen opened the door to the biology lab. Biology was a subject she liked. They did cool things in this class, and she liked learning about how life worked.

As she walked toward her seat, Gwen saw her friend Cody sitting with Justin. "I can't wait to cut into that frog!" Justin was saying. "It is going to be so cool!"

Gwen noticed that Cody looked a bit green. "Yeah," he mumbled. "It'll be great."

Gwen shot Cody a look. She knew that Cody hated the sight of blood. Also, he loved animals of all kinds. Cody returned her look with a sick smile and stared down at his desk.

It was frog day. Actually, Gwen wasn't too excited either. Why did they have to kill the frogs? The worms hadn't bothered her much, but she liked frogs.

Mrs. Brodsky had lined up the frogs under round glass hoods. She had placed bottles next to each student's lab station. The stuff in the bottles put the frogs to sleep. Mrs. Brodsky wet a cotton ball with stuff from the bottle and stuck it under the glass hood. Pretty soon her frog keeled over, fast asleep. *Ugh*, thought Gwen. *I don't want to do this.*

Gwen walked to her lab station and leaned over to look at her frog. It had dark green and brown stripes, thin yellow lines, and yellow circles around its eyes. She put her nose next to the glass. The frog stared back at her, the skin of its throat moving in and out. She picked up the cotton ball and put the liquid on it. Down the row she could hear Cody talking to his frog. He sounded totally miserable.

"Come on, everyone. If you don't put that cotton ball under the glass, we'll never get to cutting these fellows up," said Mrs. Brodsky. Gwen looked at her classmates. Most of them looked as reluctant as she felt.

Gwen sighed and tilted the hood to stick the cotton ball under it. The frog stared at her, unblinking. Soon it would be dead, just so she could know what its liver and its heart looked like. Suddenly Gwen felt a streak of rebellion. "No!" she said aloud, "I won't!" She picked up the glass hood and poked her frog. "Be free!" she shouted. Her frog took a leap and landed on the floor. Gwen raced toward the classroom door and threw it open.

All of a sudden she noticed that her classmates were doing the same thing. Everyone was poking the frogs to make them jump away. Everyone was shouting. Gwen saw Cody pick up his frog and let it jump out the open window. Frogs were hopping all over the classroom and down the hallway. It was total chaos.

Grades 7–8   *Scholastic Teaching Resources*

5

"Gwendolyn Boyd!" Mrs. Brodsky roared over the noise. Her face was a strange shade of purple. "What in the world are you thinking?"

Gwen walked over to Mrs. Brodsky. "I'm sorry, Mrs. Brodsky," Gwen answered. "I just couldn't do it. I didn't expect everyone else to let theirs go, too."

Mrs. Brodsky took a deep breath as her face began to turn back to its normal color. "All right," she said more calmly. "You will receive a zero for today."

Gwen nodded. That was fair. She had ruined the class.

"And," Mrs. Brodsky said, "you will spend your free time looking for those frogs. They are probably in every corner of the school by now. I do not want them jumping out of a corner in the middle of Mr. Cree's English class. He screams at the sight of frogs. When you have found 30 frogs, minus the one Cody let out the window, you may take them to the park and let them go. I think we have had more than enough of frogs in this class for the year!"

"Thank you, Mrs. Brodsky," Gwen said. Cody stood there smiling broadly. "I'll help!" he said, "and I bet some other kids will too."

"Good, I'll need the help," said Gwen as she walked down the hall, headed for English with Mr. Cree. She wondered how she would keep from giggling through the whole class as she waited to see a frog jump out right at his feet. School should be this exciting every day!

1. In the fourth paragraph, why did Cody look at Gwen?

Ⓐ She called his name.

Ⓑ She tapped him on the shoulder.

Ⓒ She shot him a look.

Ⓓ He hated the sight of blood.

2. Why did Mrs. Brodsky's frog keel over, fast asleep?

_____

3. What caused the frogs to jump away?

Ⓐ poking them   Ⓒ wet cotton balls

Ⓑ noise   Ⓓ saying, "Be free!"

4. Why did Gwen receive a zero?

_____

5. What is one thing that causes Mr. Cree to scream?

_____

Passage 2   Author's Purpose and Point of View

On Being Yourself

Everyone likes to feel that he or she is special. Unfortunately, many of us grow up believing that we're not special at all. We wish that we could be better at sports or more attractive. We wish we had nicer clothes or more money. Like the Scarecrow, the Tin Man, or the Cowardly Lion from *The Wizard of Oz*, we believe we're not good enough just as we are. In the movie, the Scarecrow wishes that he had a brain. The Tin Man wishes he had a heart, and the Lion wants courage. In the end, each of them realizes that he already has what he needs.

Most parents want us to be the best we can be. They sometimes try to encourage us to do better by comparing us to others. They mean well, but the message we often get is that we're not good enough. We begin to believe that the only way we can be special is by being better than someone else, but we are often disappointed. There will always be someone out there who is better than we are at something. There are plenty of people around who may not be as smart as we are but who are better at sports. Or they may not be as good-looking, but they have more money. It is impossible for us to be better than everyone else all the time.

Like the Scarecrow, the Tin Man, and the Cowardly Lion, we all want what we believe will make us better people. What we don't realize is that often we already have inside us the very things that we seek. Parents sometimes forget to tell us that we *are* special, that we are good enough just as we are. Maybe no one told them when *they* were growing up, or maybe they just forgot. Either way, it's up to us to remind them from time to time that each of us, in our own way, is special. What we are is enough.

1. **This essay was most likely written by a —**

    Ⓐ young person.   Ⓒ teacher.

    Ⓑ parent.   Ⓓ coach.

2. **The author of this essay believes that —**

    Ⓐ not everyone can be special.

    Ⓑ smart people are more special than others.

    Ⓒ the richer you are, the better you are.

    Ⓓ we are all good enough just the way we are.

3. **Why does the author discuss characters from *The Wizard of Oz* in this essay? What point is the author trying to make?**

    _____

    _____

Passage 3   Sequence

SNIP, SNIP

Angela hurried in the front door and headed for the stairs, clutching a plastic bag in her hand.

"Let's see what you bought at the mall," Mom called from the kitchen.

"No, I'd rather not show you yet," Angela replied. "Wait till I try them on."

"Well, now I know it's something to wear," her mother teased. "I can't wait to see what you picked out, and Grandma will want to know how you spent your birthday money too."

Angela closed her bedroom door, dropped the bag on her bed, and kicked off her sneakers. She pulled on the new pair of jeans. Then she looked in the mirror. *They fit perfectly,* she thought. *Just a teeny bit too long, but I know how to fix that.*

Quietly, Angela walked down the hall to Mom's bedroom and found a pair of sharp scissors next to the sewing machine. Angela picked them up carefully and carried them back to her room. Then, she cut into the fabric at the bottom of her jeans. Slowly she began to trim an inch of cloth from the bottom edge of the left leg. When the front was done, she twisted her leg, trying to reach the back. I guess I'll have to take them off, she thought.

With the jeans in her lap, Angela finished trimming an inch from the bottom of the left leg. Then she put the pants on again and looked in the mirror. She had done a good job. The cut leg looked nice and even, but it was still a bit too long.

I'll do the second leg now and make it a little shorter, Angela thought. Then I'll redo the first leg. She carefully cut two inches from the bottom of the right leg. But when she tried the jeans on, they still looked long. By this time, Angela was becoming impatient. She took off the jeans, grabbed the scissors, and cut off two more inches from the right leg. Now the right leg was shorter by four inches!

"Oh, no!" cried Angela when she looked at herself in the mirror and saw that the right leg was way too short. She could never wear the jeans now! What would she tell Grandma?

"My, you are slow! Aren't you changed yet?" called her mother from downstairs.

Angela quickly took off the new jeans. She got a ruler and, with white chalk, drew two lines on the jeans. Here goes nothing, she thought, and cut along the lines. Then Angela put the new jeans on once more and ran down the stairs . . . wearing shorts!

1. What did Angela do first in this story?
- Ⓐ She tried on her new jeans.
- Ⓑ She hurried in the front door.
- Ⓒ She spoke to her mother.
- Ⓓ She closed her bedroom door.

2. What did Angela do right after she closed the door and kicked off her sneakers?
- Ⓐ She pulled on her new jeans.
- Ⓑ She headed for the stairs.
- Ⓒ She cut the left leg.
- Ⓓ She spent her birthday money.

3. Before Angela cut the first piece from her jeans, she _____.
- Ⓐ showed the jeans to Mom
- Ⓑ put them on for the second time
- Ⓒ carried scissors to her room
- Ⓓ drew a line with chalk

4. When did Angela use a ruler?
- Ⓐ before she did any cutting at all
- Ⓑ after she went downstairs
- Ⓒ before looking in the mirror
- Ⓓ after she cut the jeans too short

5. Tell what Angela did to her jeans by writing the steps she took in the correct order.

_____

_____

_____

_____

Passage 4   Making Inferences and Predictions

On Top of the World

July 15

Dear Mom,

   We climbed up to Baxter Peak, at the top of Mount Katahdin. That's the highest peak in Maine. Joni, my counselor snapped a photo of each of us as we reached the summit. She took a group shot, too. I'll show you the photos when I get home.

   The night before our climb, Joni told us about the different trails on Katahdin. We talked about them and then took a vote on our route. Most of us wanted to go up the Knife Edge trail, which is really difficult. In some places the trail is only a few feet wide and the ground slopes down steeply on both sides. The drop is about 2,000 feet—and this goes on for a mile!

   I voted for the Knife Edge because it's the most famous trail on the mountain. Still, when the votes were counted, I was pretty nervous. I really wondered if I could manage it.

   Well, the photos are living proof that I did! It was an amazing experience. We got up at 5:00 in the morning. We knew it would be a long day. I think everyone was a bit nervous—even Lee. The counselors had done this dozens of times before. They were excited, but not nervous. They told us over and over that we could do it, no sweat. Joni took me aside and said, "You are well prepared for this climb. You can do it, and you will love it!" She was right. I did love it, and I'll never forget what a great feeling it was to reach the top.

   To reach the Knife Edge, we started out on the Chimney Pond Trail, which was easy at first. It got more rugged as we climbed, and before long we were clambering up and over huge boulders. On the Knife Edge, we inched our way along carefully. We had to go single file. That's how narrow the trail was. I was shaking, but I made it! All 12 of us made it. I think these guys are going to be my best friends for life after what we went through together!

   It was a clear day, and the view from the top was spectacular. We stopped, rested, ate, and gazed at the view for about an hour. Then Joni reminded us that it would take us another six hours to get back down.

   I'll have lots more to tell when I see you. Don't worry, Mom. I am taking good care of myself.

   Love,
   Cary

Scholastic Teaching Resources   **Grades 7-8**

1. **Where do you think Cary was when she wrote this letter?**

   Ⓐ at her best friend's house

   Ⓑ at school

   Ⓒ at summer camp

   Ⓓ at Joni's house

2. **You can guess that Cary's friend Lee usually is _____.**

   Ⓐ shy

   Ⓑ confident

   Ⓒ nervous

   Ⓓ smart

3. **Why do you think the counselors kept telling the group that they could do it?**

   Ⓐ because the group didn't listen the first time

   Ⓑ because the counselors forgot that they'd already told them

   Ⓒ so the group wouldn't be scared

   Ⓓ to make sure everyone could hear them

4. **Why do you think Cary was shaking on the Knife Edge?**

   _____

   _____

5. **When Cary returns home, what will she probably do first?**

   _____

   _____

   _____

Name _____ Date _____

The Dog for You

Are you thinking about getting a dog? Find the dog that's right for you!

Dachshund
Height: 5–9"
Weight: 9–32 lbs.
small, muscular dog
with short legs and short
hair; cheerful; good
with children;
good watchdog;
good for apartments

Doberman Pinscher
Height: 24–28"
Weight: 66–88 lbs.
short, thick hair; long legs;
muscular body; smart; aggressive;
good watchdog; not good
with small children or
in apartments

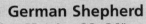

German Shepherd
Height: 22–26"
Weight: 60–95 lbs.
strong; sheds fur often; owners
must vacuum often; smart; trains
easily; obeys; good with children;
good watchdog; not for
small apartments

Old English Sheepdog
Height: 20–24"
Weight: about 66 lbs.
strong body; long, thick coat
must be brushed often to avoid
snarls; good with children; good
at herding; not for
small apartments

Soft-Coated Wheaten Terrier
Height: 17–20"
Weight: 30–45 lbs.
strong, muscular dog; fine in bad
weather; long, thick, wavy coat;
good hunting and herding dog;
good in apartments; not for
small children

Welsh Terrier
Height: 14–15.5"
Weight: 20–21 lbs.
coat must be brushed often;
good for apartments;
good watchdog

12

1. **Which breed is the tallest?**

   (A) German shepherd

   (B) Old English sheepdog

   (C) Welsh terrier

   (D) Doberman pinscher

2. **Name three breeds that are good for apartments.**

   _____

   _____

3. **Name four breeds that make good watchdogs.**

   _____

   _____

4. **If you want a dog with short hair that is cheerful, which breed would probably be best?**

   (A) German shepherd

   (B) Old English sheepdog

   (C) Welsh terrier

   (D) Dachshund

5. **Name three breeds that would be good for a family with children.**

   _____

   _____

Writing Prompt: **On a separate sheet of paper, write a paragraph telling which breed you think you'd like most and which you'd like least. Use details to explain your choices.**

Passage 6   Making Inferences and Predictions

The Snowball

Bik woke up with a feeling of excitement. It was the first day of winter and that meant snow. Bik watched the first large flakes fall on the green grass.

Bik dashed out in his bare feet and pajamas. He grabbed a handful of snow and tried to form it into a ball, but it kept falling apart. The government just couldn't get the formula right. He'd seen kids making snowballs in old movies.

Mr. King came strolling down the street.

"Oh, brother," thought Bik, "here come stories of the good old days."

"Before global warming, we used to have real snow!" exclaimed Mr. King.

"Did you always have it precisely on the first day of winter?" asked Bik.

"No," admitted Mr. King, "but snow was cold, and we had to dress warmly."

"Was it fun to throw snowballs?" asked Bik.

Mr. King nodded. "I'll be right back," he said. Several minutes later he returned with something in his mittened hand. The mitten was wet and dark.

"What's that?" asked Bik.

"It's an authentic American snowball," said Mr. King. "It's probably the last in America. It's been in my freezer for over 20 years, but I want you to have it."

"Thanks!" said Bik, taking the snowball. "Can I do whatever I want with it?"

Mr. King grinned. "I presume you know what snowballs are for," he said.

Bik eyed the side of the house.

1. When does this story take place?

   Ⓐ thousands of years ago

   Ⓑ hundreds of years ago

   Ⓒ today

   Ⓓ in the future

2. What is strange about the weather in this story?

_____

3. What will Bik probably do next?

   Ⓐ throw the snowball at the house

   Ⓑ eat the snowball

   Ⓒ throw the snowball at Mr. King

   Ⓓ put it in his freezer

River Raft Adventure!

Everyone loves rafting! Just ask any of the rafting guides at River Raft Adventures (RRA). RRA has been guiding trips since 1993. We are the best rafting company in the West. All of our guides are highly trained and ready to share the thrill of river rafting with you.

If you have been rafting before and are seeking a challenge, we have just the right trip for you. If you are ready to "test the waters" with your very first white-water run, take a trip with us.

- A guide rides on each raft. Our guides are the friendliest in the business.

- Every passenger is part of the crew and helps to paddle under the guide's direction.

- We have trips lasting from 1 to 5 days.

- We provide all meals and they are delicious.

- There are comfortable cabins for overnight trips.

- All trips have beautiful views.

"I have been a rafting guide since 1988. Rafting is relaxing and also exciting. Choose the trip that you like best. You will have a wonderful time!"
Mac Summers, guide

"I loved my rafting trip. It was challenging and fun. The crew was great. They worked as a team with the help of our guide. It was peaceful and beautiful along the river. I have recommended the trip to many of my friends."
Karen Cho, customer

**Call or e-mail RRA today. RRA will answer your questions
by phone or e-mail. Let us help you plan your next adventure.**

telephone: 296-8496 • email: tomasin@riverraftadventure.net

1. **Which idea from this advertisement is a fact?**

   Ⓐ Everyone loves rafting!

   Ⓑ RRA has trips lasting from 1 day to 5 days.

   Ⓒ Rafting is thrilling.

   Ⓓ Rafting is relaxing.

2. **Which of Karen Cho's statements is a fact?**

   Ⓐ "I have recommended the trip to many of my friends."

   Ⓑ "The crew was great."

   Ⓒ "It was peaceful and beautiful along the river."

   Ⓓ "It was challenging and fun."

3. **Which idea from this passage is an opinion?**

   Ⓐ A guide rides on each raft.

   Ⓑ RRA will answer your questions by phone or e-mail.

   Ⓒ RRA has the perfect trip for you.

   Ⓓ RRA has been guiding rafting trips since 1993.

4. **Which sentence states a fact?**

   Ⓐ RRA is the best rafting company in the West.

   Ⓑ RRA provides meals.

   Ⓒ RRA guides are the friendliest in the business.

   Ⓓ All meals are delicious.

5. **Write one fact and one opinion expressed by Mac Summers in this ad.**

   _____

   _____

   _____

   _____

16

To the Editor:

Let Everyone Play!

Dear Editor,

I am an eighth-grade student at Central Middle School. In my three years at the school I have played soccer, basketball, and baseball. I love sports and really enjoy being part of a team. Playing on our school sports teams has been the best part of middle school for me. I know I'm lucky that I've had this opportunity.

Some kids have not been so lucky. In fact, many kids who love sports don't have the chance to play on a school team. That's because, to make a team, you have to try out. The idea is that kids who are good at sports will do well in tryouts and make the team. But what about the kids who don't do well during tryouts? Maybe they are ill that day, or nervous, or are just having a bad day, so they don't play their best. They don't make the team, and that is unfair.

Also, there are kids who really don't have the skills to play well. They never make a team, and that isn't fair either. How will kids ever learn the skills if they don't have a chance to play? Remember, this is school and students

> **Remember, this is school and students are here to learn. All kids should have the chance to learn sports skills and teamwork by playing on a school sports team.**

are here to learn. All kids should have the chance to learn sports skills and teamwork by playing on a school sports team.

There are other reasons why every student should have the chance to play sports. Sports are important for good health and fitness. They help kids feel good about themselves and their school. They build friendships among teammates. Coaches are good role models, and students who play team sports learn good sportsmanship. And, most important, team sports are fun! Players have fun playing, and their parents have fun watching and cheering for the team. So, sports bring kids and parents together, too.

By now you know how I feel. Every kid who wants to play on a school sports team should have the chance. These teams are for fun and fitness—they're not professional teams! Let's change the rules for making a team. Let's get rid of tryouts. Let's give every student at Central Middle School the chance to wear a team uniform.

Mike Fuji

1. **Mike Fuji's main purpose for writing this letter was to _____.**

   (A) brag about playing three different sports

   (B) tell about exciting moments on the basketball court and baseball field

   (C) persuade girls and boys to try out for a school team

   (D) convince people that all students should be able to play on school teams

2. **The writer believes that tryouts are _____.**

   (A) a bother

   (B) useful

   (C) unfair

   (D) fun

3. **In Mike's opinion, school sports teams should be for _____.**

   (A) learning skills and teamwork

   (B) showing off the best players

   (C) professional athletes

   (D) making the school famous

4. **Name the reason that Mike thinks is the most important for playing team sports.**

   _____

5. **Mike hopes that his letter will _____.**

   (A) raise money to buy more uniforms

   (B) allow more kids to play team sports

   (C) get parents to practice sports skills

   (D) stop school sports

   Writing Prompt: **On a separate sheet of paper, write a letter to the editor in response to Mike's letter. First decide on your point of view and your purpose for writing. (Do you agree with Mike and support his ideas, or do you feel differently?) Express your views in your letter.**

Scholastic Teaching Resources   **Grades 7-8**

SCHOOL UNIFORMS?
Think Again!

At Tuesday's meeting of the school teacher–parent team, Mr. Russell made his position clear. He wants the children in our city's public schools to wear school uniforms. "Uniforms make life easier for families," he said. Parents do not have to decide what kind of clothes to buy for school. And, it's easier to get ready for school each day. "Uniforms help children feel better about themselves," he added. Children from poor families wear the same clothes as children from rich families. Uniforms make it easier for children of different backgrounds to make friends.

His suggestion sparked a lively debate. Two parents, Stan Oakley and Mae Stokes, said they thought it was a good idea. Mr. Oakley suggested that the schools would look much neater. Children's behavior might even improve.

Others were not so sure. "Is there a problem now?" asked Gary Washington. "I wasn't aware that this was an issue."

And, it's easier to get ready for school each day.

Indeed, what is the issue? What problem is our superintendent trying to solve? Would children really feel better about themselves if they had to wear clothes that someone else picked out? Americans like to express themselves through their clothes. Uniforms can crush creativity. Paying for uniforms might be hard for some families. They would have to pay for the uniform no matter what it costs. Then they would need to buy other clothes for their children to wear outside of school.

Mr. Russell has asked the school team to vote for his plan. Clearly, this city is not ready to make a decision yet. We need more information. The school team should interview students, parents, and teachers in towns that have school uniforms. They should do research to find out the cost of uniforms. Then they should hold public meetings to discuss their findings. It would be foolish to rush into a vote on this question.

1. **Which of these sentences is a fact?**

    Ⓐ Uniforms help children feel better about themselves.

    Ⓑ Americans like to express themselves through their clothes.

    Ⓒ Mr. Russell has asked the school team to vote for his plan.

    Ⓓ It would be foolish to rush into a vote on this question.

2. **Why does Mr. Russell think school uniforms are a good idea? List two reasons.**

_____

_____

_____

3. **Which reason supports Mr. Oakley's opinion about school uniforms?**

    Ⓐ Paying for uniforms might be hard for some families.

    Ⓑ People don't get to express themselves when they wear uniforms.

    Ⓒ Uniforms are dull.

    Ⓓ Schools would look neater and children would behave better.

4. **What is the writer's opinion of school uniforms? How can you tell?**

_____

_____

_____

5. **What is your own opinion on school uniforms? Give reasons for your opinion.**

_____

_____

_____

Passage 10   Drawing Conclusions

Meet a Snowboard Champ

This week Kids and Sports *magazine interviewed snowboard enthusiast Steve Glass. Steve has been snowboarding for five years. Last month, Steve was in the ISF Junior World Championships.*

Kids and Sports: Steve, how did you get started snowboarding?

Steve: Well, I learned to ski when I was pretty small. I loved skiing, but when I started to see the tricks that snowboarders could do, I knew that was the sport for me. And I love competing.

Kids and Sports: Of course, most snowboarders don't compete. They are in the sport for the fun of it.

Steve: That's right. Enjoying the beauty of the mountain with friends—there's nothing like it.

Kids and Sports: Steve, do you have some advice for kids who are interested in trying the sport?

Steve: Sure. It's important to have the right equipment. It's a good idea to rent first. Beginners should get a freestyle board, which is shorter, wider, and more flexible than a race board. Choose boots and bindings that work together. Soft boots are for freestyle riding. You won't need a hard boot unless you take up racing later on.

Kids and Sports: What about clothing?

Steve: Just wear a jacket that's long and loose. Snowboard pants are a good idea; get the kind with padding at the knees and bottom. You will be glad you did!

Kids and Sports: Anything else?

story continued on page 22...

21

Grades 7-8   **Scholastic Teaching Resources**

Steve: Always wear a hat, gloves that won't fall off, and sunglasses or goggles. And don't forget sunscreen.

Kids and Sports: Okay. Now, how about some hints about what to do out on the mountain?

Steve: Well, first you should practice moving on flat ground. Then try walking uphill. Practice falling, both forward and backward. To do this, try to relax and keep your arms tucked close to your body. Getting up is tricky for beginners, so practice that, too. Have someone show you the basic riding position and a few different turns. Then, when you know all that, you may want to try some ground tricks and spins.

Kids and Sports: Thanks, Steve. I'm sure our readers can't wait to get to the slopes. Anything else?

Steve: Yes. Have a great time, and always keep your leash attached so you don't lose your board!

1. **Why do you think Steve says it's a good idea to rent equipment first?**

   _____

   _____

2. **Why do you think Steve suggests getting special snowboard pants?**
   - Ⓐ If you don't have them, people will know you're a beginner.
   - Ⓑ You have to buy them because you can't rent clothing.
   - Ⓒ They are required equipment for the sport.
   - Ⓓ The padding in them will help protect you when you fall.

3. **Why do you think Steve suggests snowboarders wear sunglasses or goggles and use sunscreen?**

   _____

   _____

4. **Steve suggests that you use a leash with your board. To what two things do you think the leash is attached?**

   _____

   _____

5. **What can you tell about Steve Glass from this interview?**
   - Ⓐ He's a good student.
   - Ⓑ He always snowboards with his best friend.
   - Ⓒ He knows a lot about snowboarding.
   - Ⓓ He writes for a magazine.

22

Passage 11   Cause and Effect

The Mysterious
"BLACK BOX"

When an airplane crashes, the first thing people do is ask, "What went wrong? How can we keep it from happening again?" At this point, someone will mention the "black box." Actually, an airplane's black box is orange. Because the box is bright orange, it is easier for people to find the box after a crash. All commercial airplanes must carry the boxes, and because of this, air safety has improved.

What is a black box? A black box is a powerful data collection device. You may have heard of an airplane's flight data recorder (FDR) and cockpit voice recorder (CVR). The cockpit is the area in front where the pilot sits. Together, these record up to 300 different kinds of information about a flight. For example, they record an airplane's speed and altitude. Also, they record everything the pilots say to each other and over the radio. This helps people piece together just what happened in the minutes before a crash.

In what part of the airplane is a black box placed? Many people are surprised to learn that black boxes are not found up front in the cockpit. Instead, they are housed in the airplane's tail.

How do the recording devices inside a black box survive a crash? The boxes are made of very strong materials. They are very well insulated, too. This protects the devices in two ways. It gives protection from the crash itself. And it protects against very high heat and fire.

Why are black boxes so well protected? Black boxes record important information. Without them, many questions about an accident could never be answered. The information helps people understand and explain what went wrong. As a result, airplane designers can make changes so the problem will not happen again.

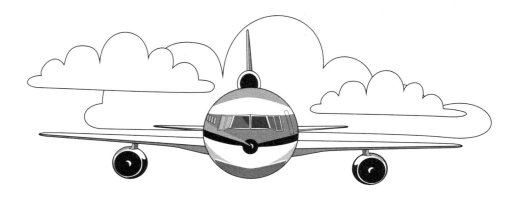

23

1. **The "black boxes" on airplanes are colored orange to _____.**

   (A) hide them in the airplane's tail
   (B) make them easier to find
   (C) protect them against heat
   (D) make them stronger

2. **What has resulted from airplanes carrying black boxes?**

   (A) There are now more crashes.
   (B) Pilots can't talk over the radio.
   (C) Air safety has improved.
   (D) Airplanes never have accidents.

3. **Why wouldn't a black box be destroyed by most fires in a crash?**

   (A) A black box is very well insulated.
   (B) People need to study it.
   (C) It is in the tail, not the cockpit.
   (D) It is colored orange instead of black.

4. **What can airplane designers do with the information gathered from black boxes?**

   _____

   _____

   _____

5. **What would be one effect of not having a black box in an airplane?**

   _____

   _____

   _____

Name _____

Ronnie's Restaurant Review

VOLUME XXV   Warrenville, USA   **January 10, 2004**

Big Bite Burgers

Last week I decided to try something different from my usual salad and sandwich lunch places. So I went to Big Bite Burgers.

Big Bite opened a month ago and is already very popular. It's easy to see why. The atmosphere is fun and the food is good. If you're looking for fancy, this isn't it. It has fun red-and-white booths and stools set at a long counter. Music, from old rock to today's hits, plays throughout the restaurant adding to the atmosphere.

We started off with shakes. My vanilla shake was perfect—smooth and creamy. The chocolate shake was wonderful too. The strawberry shake was too sweet and did not taste like real strawberries.

The burgers were just what burgers should be—thick and not too dry with just a little grease. (This is not a place for those trying to eat light. The veggie burger is so-so, and the salads are ho-hum: lettuce with tomato and bottled dressing.)

I ordered the Mushroom-Swiss burger. The mushrooms were fresh and the cheese was lightly melted. The Big Blue, a burger with bacon and blue cheese, also tasted great. The Ham 'n Swisser is a good choice for those who don't want a burger. So is the Gobbler, a turkey sandwich with cranberries. Skip the Mexican burger. The salsa tasted store-bought, and the burger's tortilla chips got soggy.

As for side dishes, go for the fries. They're perfectly cooked with very little grease. Other sides, like coleslaw, are fine, but the fries are too good to miss.

Big Bite Burgers is a block from the theaters on Seventh Street. Stop in early for dinner before a movie or after the movie for one of their great desserts.

---

1. **The author's main purpose in writing this selection was to _____.**
   - (A) give directions to Big Bite Burgers
   - (B) evaluate a new restaurant for her readers
   - (C) tell dieters they should not go to Big Bite Burgers
   - (D) compliment the new restaurant for its good food

2. **Overall, what is the author's view of Big Bite Burgers?**
   - (A) She thinks all the food needs improvement.
   - (B) She thinks that people on diets should go there to eat.
   - (C) She very much likes the atmosphere and most of the food.
   - (D) She finds it fun and enjoyable but likes fancier restaurants.

3. **List at least two things that Ronnie did not like at Big Bite Burgers.**

   _____

   _____

Passage 13   Steps in a Process

Making a Sled Kite

$\mathcal{K}$ites have been part of many different cultures for thousands of years. They have also been used for many reasons. For example, scientists who study weather use kites. In the 1700s, Ben Franklin tied a metal key to the tail of a kite. He flew it during a thunderstorm. When lightning hit it, he learned about electricity.

Today, we're going to make a kite just for fun. So let's get to it. First get all the materials you need together. Then follow the steps below.

- 12-by-17-inch (or larger) cardboard or foam board
- craft knife
- 12-by-17-inch brown bag paper, white drawing paper, or colored wrapping paper
- pencil
- scissors
- markers, crayons, glitter paint, and tissue paper

- clear packing tape
- hole punch
- two 16-inch long (1/8-inch-wide) wooden sticks
- 21-foot (or longer) ball of flying string on spool
- ruler
- 2-inch-by-2-foot streamer

STEP 1: Make a pattern for your kite out of cardboard or foam board. Use a craft knife to cut out the shape as shown in Figure 1.

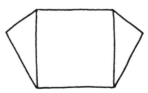

Fig. 1

STEP 2: Use the pattern as a guide for cutting out your kite shape. Put the paper under the pattern and trace around it. Then cut along the traced lines.

STEP 3: Next, decorate your kite.

STEP 4: Reinforce the wing tips by putting a piece of tape over each one. You may want to use two or three pieces of tape to make the wing tip stronger. Then, punch a hole in each wing tip as shown in Figure 2.

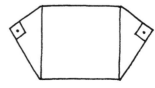

Fig. 2

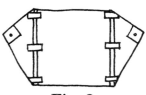

Fig. 3

STEP 5: Attach the wooden sticks along each wing fold with packing tape. Fold any edges of tape that stick out over the wings. Make sure the tape folds over the sticks as shown in Figure 3.

STEP 6: Tie a piece of string (about one foot long) to the holes in the wing tips. Leave a little slack in the string. Make a loop in the center of the string as shown in Figure 4. This is called the bridle.

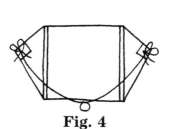

Fig. 4

STEP 7: Attach the streamer to the bottom of the kite with tape. This is the "tail."

STEP 8: Tie the string to the loop in the bridle.

STEP 9: Now, go fly a kite!

1. **What is the first thing you should do after gathering the materials together?**
   - Ⓐ Make a pattern.
   - Ⓑ Cut the shape out of a piece of paper.
   - Ⓒ Use a craft knife to cut cardboard.
   - Ⓓ Make the bridle.

2. **What is the second step?**

   _____

   _____

3. **What should you do just before you put tape over the wing tips?**

   _____

   _____

4. **After you have punched a hole in each wing tip, what should you do next?**

   _____

   _____

5. **What is the last thing you should do before you fly your kite?**

   _____

   _____

27

Name _____   Date _____

It's a Wild and Wonderful Ride, But Is It Safe?

by Akiko Ono

The Cyclone, Kumba, Superman, Space Mountain, the SooperDooperLooper, the Great American Scream Machine, the Corkscrew . . . What do these names have in common? They're all roller coasters at American amusement parks.

Roller coasters are the most popular rides at most amusement parks. These days, each new coaster built has to be bigger, faster, more exciting, and scarier than the last. But how do riders know the coasters are safe?

What do parks do to test their coasters before we excitedly jump into a car, fasten our belts, and take that ride?

Parks are very careful about testing their coasters. They have to make sure that the coaster does not go too fast and that the loops and turns are not too tight. They also have to make sure that riders will not get sick or hurt. They use computer models to make sure the design is safe. The models show, for example, that the coaster won't fly off the track or send riders shooting into midair. They test the coasters with water dummies of different sizes that represent real riders. Then they study the effects of the coaster ride on the dummies. They use crash test dummies, like carmakers do, to measure the stress the coaster puts on human bodies. Finally, they run the ride over and over with real test riders. What a great job that sounds like—riding roller coasters all day!

Actually, it's probably not as fun as it sounds. Think about it. Your body is jolted around, your stomach drops, and the turns and loops make you dizzy—all day long. Some parks hire volunteers to come in and ride all day. One such rider, when interviewed, said, "When I was asked if I wanted to be a test rider, I jumped at the chance. And the first six or seven times were great! But by the thirtieth time, I was so ready to get off that ride. I felt sick and had a headache. And frankly, the ride was boring by then."

28

Parks also hire full-time testers. These people ride new roller coasters many times before the coasters open. One test rider says, "By the way, it's not a good idea to eat a big meal just before you test coasters." No kidding! The same tester remembers how once when a new coaster opened, he rode it 23 times in a row. The rest of his day wasn't so great.

Testers learn each coaster well. They can hear any little new sound or feel any new

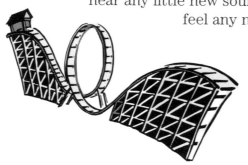

bump or jolt the coaster makes. Several times a week, they ride each coaster to check for anything that seems different or that concerns them. If they notice anything, however small, they let the people who repair the coaster know. The staff then goes over the coaster to make sure there is nothing wrong with it.

Full-time testers seem to love their jobs, even if there is the occasional day of feeling sick. They never get over the rush that comes when they turn upside down, drop 80 feet, and twist through turns. For these thrill-seekers, coasters never get boring. For the rest of us, the testers are the last step in making sure our rides are safe as well as fun and exciting.

1. **What is the main idea of this article?**
   Ⓐ Each new coaster has to be bigger, faster, more exciting, and scarier.
   Ⓑ Amusement parks test their roller coasters for safety.
   Ⓒ Working as a full-time roller coaster tester can be very tiring.
   Ⓓ Roller coaster test riders are thrill-seekers who love riding coasters.

2. **Which detail best supports the idea that test-riding a new roller coaster might not be as fun as it sounds?**
   Ⓐ One such rider, when interviewed, said, "When I was asked if I wanted to be a test rider, I jumped at the chance."
   Ⓑ These people ride new roller coasters many times before the coasters open.
   Ⓒ The models show that the coaster won't fly off the track or send riders shooting into midair.
   Ⓓ Your body is jolted around, your stomach drops, and the turns and loops make you dizzy—all day long.

3. **List two details from this passage to support the idea that testers learn each coaster well.**

   _____

   _____

29

Passage 15 Drawing Conclusions

Isabel Leaves a Trail of Destruction

by Anna Ruiz

Outer Banks, N.C.
Sept. 19, 2003

It looks like a war zone. Apartment buildings have whole walls ripped off. You can see the rain-soaked furniture inside. Cars and trucks lie flipped on their sides. Glass from broken windows sparkles in the streets. Roads have fallen into the sea.

Since Isabel hit the Atlantic coast, more than three million people have lost power. Airlines have canceled almost 5,700 flights. Washington, D.C., has been shut down.

Stray pets roam the streets. Animal lovers have set up emergency shelters. They feed the animals and treat their cuts. They take photos and post them on a board. People stop by and study the board to see if their pet dog or cat has ended up here.

People cry when they see their ruined houses. They say, "It could've been worse. At least we're safe."

The houses can be rebuilt. Insurance will pay for new trailers and new cars. But what about the trees that are down? Some trees that are standing have no leaves. A leaf is no match for winds that can blow a roof off.

Some of the people who survived the storm are packing up for good. They say they're leaving the North Carolina coast. They don't want to live in hurricane country any more.

Others are planning to rebuild. This time, they say, the houses will be better made and will be fitted with storm shutters. And next time the weather report says a hurricane is coming, homeowners will close those shutters to keep the wind from tearing into the house.

---

1. **What do you think created all the destruction described in this article?**

    Ⓐ a person
    Ⓑ a hurricane
    Ⓒ a flood
    Ⓓ a monster

2. **Why do you think so many flights were canceled?**

    _____

3. **Do you think there have been hurricanes in North Carolina before this one? Why or why not?**

    _____

    _____

Passage 16   Story Elements

Stick-to-it-ive Brian

Brian looked at the ugly gray walls of his bedroom. Soon the hated walls would be covered, but not with paint as he had first planned. Brian had been disappointed to learn that the landlord would not allow painting. For weeks he had puzzled over the problem: without using paint, how could he cover the walls? But, as Grandmother always said, "Necessity is the mother of invention." So Brian did some thinking, and with a little help from his mother, he came up with a great plan.

This morning, Mom had needed to stop at the mall to buy a book and Brian went along. While Mom looked through the books, Brian noticed a large poster of Harry Potter and the Hogwarts School on the wall. Next to it was a poster showing the cover of *No Arm in Left Field*, a baseball novel by Matt Christopher that Brian had read several times. This is it, Brian thought excitedly. I'll cover the walls with posters!

Mom thought it was a great idea too. "Why don't you look in the store that sells baseball cards?" she suggested. "I'll bet they sell posters of ball players."

When they left the mall, Brian had an armful of posters and a box of tacks. At home, he headed straight to his room. First he unrolled the posters and spread them out on his bed, his desk, and most of the floor. Next he measured each poster, and then he measured the walls. He wanted to cover as much of those ugly walls as possible! It took all afternoon to work out the best arrangement. He drew it on paper, making changes until it was just right. When Dad came home at dinnertime, Brian was ready to tack up the posters.

"Come see my room, Dad," called Brian. "It's going to be great!"

But when Dad came into the bedroom, he frowned. "The landlord said we cannot put any holes in the walls. You can't use thumbtacks, Brian. I am sorry."

Brian's joy faded. He would be stuck with the dull gray walls forever. Maybe there was no solution after all. How could you hang posters without using tacks? After all, posters would not stick to the walls by themselves!

"What would stick to the walls?" Brian wondered. Then he smiled. Tape, that's what! Brian took a piece of tape and made it into a loop. He made sure the sticky part of the tape was on the outside. This would work, for sure!

31

1. **In this story, Brian's main problem is _____.**
   - (A) getting permission to paint his room
   - (B) working out a good arrangement for his posters
   - (C) getting permission to use tacks
   - (D) finding a way to cover ugly bedroom walls

2. **Which word best describes Brian?**
   - (A) persistent
   - (B) careless
   - (C) impatient
   - (D) thoughtless

3. **What solution does Brian finally reach?**
   - (A) He decides to paint his room.
   - (B) He decides to use the tacks even though his dad tells him not to.
   - (C) He decides to use tape on the walls.
   - (D) He realizes that the gray walls are not really so bad.

4. **Which sentence expresses a theme of this story?**
   - (A) You can solve problems if you think creatively.
   - (B) Kids should be allowed to paint their rooms.
   - (C) It's fun to have a lot of posters in your bedroom.
   - (D) You should never put holes in your walls.

5. **Where does this story take place?**

   _____

   _____

Writing Prompt: **On a separate piece of paper, retell the story in your own words. Remember to include information about the time and place of the story, the characters, the problem, and how the problem is solved.**

Passage 17   Comparing and Contrasting

Blue Jeans

Loose, tight, straight-legged. What kind of jeans do you wear? Are your jeans the dark blue color? (They may not be since today you can buy jeans in light blue as well as brown, black, white, green, and even red.) There are long jeans, jean shorts, and jean skirts. People wear denim jeans for play, work, school, and parties. People of all ages— from babies on up—wear jeans, and that's not surprising. After all, jeans are comfortable and rugged. They are usually cheap except for "designer jeans."

These jeans are made by famous clothing designers. In the 1970s, many American designers began making jeans and charging high prices for them. A pair of these jeans can sell for well over $100!

In the 1850s, the first jeans cost just 22 cents. Levi Strauss, a young immigrant, invented the rugged pants. He started making the pants for miners during the California Gold Rush. At first, he used tent canvas to make his pants. Later he switched to a strong cotton fabric called *serge de Nimes*. This fabric got its name from the town of Nimes, France, and became known as "denim." Strauss used a dark dye to color the denim before it was sewn into pants.

33

In 1873 a Nevada tailor named Jacob Davis teamed up with Strauss. Davis had the idea of putting little bits of metal on the pants to stop the pockets from tearing. Miners and railroad men found the new style of pants rugged and comfortable. Pants that carried the label "Levi's" became wildly popular in the days of the Gold Rush and have remained so ever since.

---

1. What was different about the jeans Davis & Strauss made?

   Ⓐ They cost more money.

   Ⓑ They came in lots of different colors.

   Ⓒ They were more comfortable.

   Ⓓ They had little bits of metal to stop the pockets from tearing.

2. Compared with other jeans, designer jeans _____.

   Ⓐ are less rugged   Ⓒ look more comfortable

   Ⓑ cost more   Ⓓ are never blue

3. How did the price of Levi's jeans of the 1850s differ from the price of other jeans sold today?

_____

_____

_____

4. Compare and contrast the kinds of people who wore jeans in the 1850s with the kinds of people who wear jeans today.

_____

_____

_____

5. Compare and contrast the purpose of the first jeans with the purpose of jeans today.

_____

_____

_____

Name _____ Date _____

Welcome to Moviefans.com!

Have you ever sat in a theater at the end of a movie to watch the credits? As the credits rolled by, you probably saw the names of crew jobs you did not know, such as gaffers and grips. What do these people do, anyway?

It takes many people to make a movie. Each person's job is important in helping to get the movie finished, or "in the can." Below are descriptions of some of those strange-sounding jobs.

Movie Terms

best boy: The best boy is generally the assistant chief lighting technician (tech). Best boys order lighting equipment. They are in charge of the lighting crew and make sure the crew knows when it is scheduled to work.

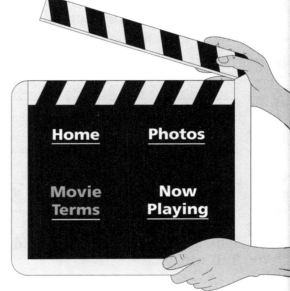

boom operator: A boom is a long pole with a microphone at the end. The boom operator holds the boom so that the microphone is in exactly the right place to pick up what the actors are saying. The point is to make sure the microphone picks up the sound clearly without getting in the picture.

gaffer: A gaffer is chief technician and aide to "important" people on the shoot, like the director. A gaffer's job is to make sure the lighting equipment is in the right place at the right time.

grip: The grip moves equipment where it needs to go. Grips build, move, set up, and fix any gear needed for the movie except the lighting equipment, which the gaffer takes care of.

swing gang: This crew builds and tears down sets. They move things like tables or chairs that are part of a set.

1. **A gaffer and best boy might work together because they both _____.**
   - Ⓐ work with lighting equipment
   - Ⓑ are chief technicians
   - Ⓒ work as assistant lighting chiefs
   - Ⓓ are chief aides to the director

2. **Look at the description of a grip's job. Do you think "grip" is a good name for someone who does this work? Why or why not?**

   _____

   _____

   _____

3. **Why do you think the boom operator tries to make sure the microphone doesn't get in the picture?**

   _____

   _____

4. **Think about what a swing gang does. Do you think "swing gang" is a good name for people who do this kind of work? Why or why not?**

   _____

   _____

5. **Which of the jobs listed would you be most interested in doing? Tell why.**

   _____

   _____

   _____

   _____

Home　　**Photos**　　**Movie Terms**　　**Now Playing**

36

Name _____ Date _____

Come Meet Our New Pals—
The Sloth Bears

ZooNooz   April 24

Have you ever heard of a sloth bear? Like sloths, sloth bears use their curved claws to hang in trees. However, sloth bears are actually a species of bear.

Sloth bears live mainly in India and Sri Lanka. Like other bears from this part of the world, sloth bears have a U-, V-, or Y-shaped white or yellow mark on their chests. Like all bears, sloth bears have thick, heavy fur. However, their dark fur is long and shaggy, which makes them look messy. In fact, sloth bears are really kind of funny-looking. While most bears have short ears, sloth bears have large, floppy ears. They also have long, pointed noses and stomachs with almost no fur.

Although some bears eat bugs, a sloth bear's diet is mostly termites. Unlike other bears, sloth bears have only 40 adult teeth. They are missing two teeth, which creates a gap inside their mouths. Like anteaters, sloth bears use their mouths as vacuums. They suck up ants or termites with a loud whoosh that can be heard hundreds of feet away!

There are a few other interesting differences between sloth bears and other bears. Sloth bears do not have a long winter's sleep. Also, a mother sloth bear carries her cubs on her back. No other bear does this. Only sloth bears can close up their nostrils at will. Sloth bears may also suck on their paws while they sleep.

But don't take our word for all of this. Come by the zoo and see our sloth bears for yourselves. They receive visitors from 9 A.M. to 6 P.M. every day.

1. **In what way are sloth bears like sloths?**

   Ⓐ They are funny-looking.

   Ⓑ They slurp up ants and termites.

   Ⓒ Their fur is shaggy and messy-looking.

   Ⓓ They use their claws to hang in trees.

2. **What is one way that sloth bears are like most other bears?**

   Ⓐ They have thick, heavy fur.

   Ⓑ They have large floppy ears.

   Ⓒ They eat mainly termites.

   Ⓓ They live only in the countries of India and Sri Lanka.

3. **List two ways in which sloth bears are different from other bears.**

   _____

   _____

Name _____ Date _____

Spiders

Spiders live in almost every corner of the world. They have been around for more than 350 million years. Clearly, they are tough creatures. Tons of people get the creeps just looking at spiders. However, spiders really are fascinating.

Web Weavers

The most interesting thing about spiders is their webs. By weight, spider silk is the strongest of all natural fibers. To make silk, spiders make a liquid inside their bodies into solid silk. A spider can spin a web with 1,500 connecting points in less than an hour. This is really amazing, and no two webs are ever the same! Each web is built to suit its location and purpose. And did you know that spiders often take their own webs apart? They absorb the silk back into their bodies. Spiders are incredible things!

Spider Silk

Spider silk doesn't dissolve in water. It doesn't react chemically with any known substance. Also, harmful bacteria don't seem to affect it. Scientists are trying to make their own silk in labs. They hope that if they can make silk that is really like spider silk, they can use it to help people. For example, the silk could be used in medicine to replace damaged tissues. Spider silk might also be useful to companies looking for a very strong material. But for now, spiders are keeping the secret of spider silk to themselves!

1. **An opinion stated in this article is _____.**

    (A) Spiders have been around for more that 350 million years.
    (B) Spider silk doesn't dissolve in water.
    (C) The most interesting thing about spiders is their webs.
    (D) Scientists are trying to make their own silk in labs.

2. **A fact stated in this article is _____.**

    (A) Spiders really are fascinating.
    (B) Tons of people get the creeps just looking at spiders.
    (C) Spiders absorb the silk back into their bodies.
    (D) Spiders are incredible things.

3. **The text states, "This is really amazing, and no two webs are ever the same!" Which part of the sentence is fact and which part is opinion?**

    _____

    _____

Scholastic Teaching Resources   **Grades 7-8**

Name _____ Date _____

**Book Review—*Darkness Over Denmark:
The Danish Resistance and the Rescue
of the Jews* by Ellen Levine**

In this excellent book for young people, the author tells why she wrote it. As a Jewish child growing up in the United States, she read many stories about World War II. During the war, Germany invaded many countries in Europe. In most countries, German soldiers rounded up the Jewish people who lived there. The Jews were sent to camps where most of them died. Denmark was different. In 1943, Danes heard of the German plan to round up Danish Jews. They did not stand by and watch. Instead, they fought back. Nearly all of the 8,000 Jews in Denmark were saved. Levine wanted to find out why the Danes acted differently from their neighbors in other countries.

Levine wanted to tell the story "through the people who experienced it." She spoke with dozens of Danes who had lived through the war. Some of them sent her information and translated for her. They felt that it was important for others to learn the story.

The book is exciting because it has many dramatic tales of rescue. For example, Jette Thing was a baby when her mother tried to escape to Sweden in a rowboat. A scared girl in the boat dropped Jette in the water. Jette's uncle jumped in and saved her. Amazing photographs from the time bring the story to life.

Many features make this book easy to use. It has a time line of important events. Levine also includes a list of all the people whose stories she told. I recommend this book to anyone interested in learning more about the strength of the human spirit.

1. Why did Ellen Levine write this book?

Ⓐ She wanted to write about World War I.

Ⓑ She wanted to find out why the Danes acted differently.

Ⓒ She wanted to translate the book into Danish.

Ⓓ She wanted to take amazing photographs.

2. Why were most Danish Jews saved?

_____

_____

3. According to the writer, what makes this book exciting?

_____

_____

Passage 22   Steps in a Process

EGG ROLLS

Did you ever wonder how to make an egg roll? Here's a simple recipe that tells you how. Egg rolls can be made with different vegetables such as carrots or mushrooms. They can also be made with meat. Egg roll wrappers may be found in grocery stores. Most wrappers are made of rice paper but some are made with wheat flour. Egg rolls are best made in a Chinese wok, but you can make them in a frying pan instead. Ask an adult to help you.

What You Need:

2 tablespoons cooking oil
2 cups shredded cabbage
2 stalks celery, minced
2 scallions or 1 onion, minced
1 cup shredded, cooked pork
or 1 cup raw, chopped shrimp

1 1/2 teaspoons salt
1/8 teaspoon black pepper
2 1/2 teaspoons sugar
8 to 10 egg roll wrappers
1 egg, beaten
3 cups cooking oil

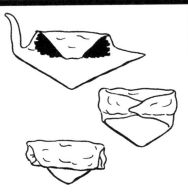

What You Do:

1. Get all ingredients ready.
2. Set the wok on the stove over high heat. Add 2 tablespoons of oil. Then stir-fry the cabbage, celery, and scallion (or onion) for 2 minutes.
3. Turn off heat. Remove the wok from the stove. Add the pork or shrimp, salt, pepper, and sugar, and mix well.
4. Fill egg roll wrappers with 1 or 2 tablespoons of filling. Do not overfill.

Fold and seal each wrapper with egg as shown. Let the egg rolls sit for 1 hour.
5. When ready to cook, heat 3 cups oil in the wok. Cook each egg roll 4 to 5 minutes or until golden brown, turning often. Drain and keep warm. Serve egg rolls warm with a dipping sauce, such as mustard or plum sauce.

1. **What is the first step?**

   _____

2. **What should you do just after you have stir-fried the vegetables for two minutes?**

   (A) Turn off the heat.   (C) Set the wok over high heat.
   (B) Add 2 tablespoons of oil.   (D) Fill the egg roll wrappers.

3. **How should egg rolls be served?**

   _____

Passage 23   Story Elements

Vote for Zach and . . .

Ant Boy
Date: Mon, 23 Aug 2004 10:44:45
Subject: Ant Boy
From: Kate <kate@yahoo.com>
To: Zach <zach@aol14.com>

I can't believe you're telling everyone that I was the person who wrote "Ant Boy" on your campaign poster.

Ant Boy
Date: Mon, 23 Aug 2004 11:39:54
Subject: Re: Ant Boy
From: Zach <zach@aol14.com>
To: Kate <kate@yahoo.com>

Who else would have written it?

Re: Ant Boy
Date: Mon, 23 Aug 2004 12:23:38
Subject: Re: Ant Boy
From: Kate <kate@yahoo.com>
To: Zach <zach@aol14.com>

Listen, Zach, I think it is really unhealthy to blame others for your problem. Aren't politicians supposed to tell their supporters about anything weird in their past? Well, I think you should have told the public that you liked to eat ants in preschool. Not everybody wants a class president who once snacked on insects! Take responsibility for your past, Zach!

Re: Ant Boy
Date: Mon, 23 Aug 2004 2:50:42
Subject: Re: Ant Boy
From: Zach <zach@aol14.com>
To: Kate <kate@yahoo.com>

What is wrong with you? Why are you acting so weird?

Re: Ant Boy
Date: Mon, 23 Aug 2004 3:02:35
Subject: Re: Ant Boy
From: Kate <kate@yahoo.com>
To: Zach <zach@aol14.com>

Zach, a true leader would have called every person in our class and asked for the truth about who wrote "Ant Boy" in a direct and sincere manner. A true leader would have persuaded the culprit to confess and help him (that's you) make new posters before the election next week. A true leader would have asked his best friend (that's me) to run with him as vice president.

Re: Ant Boy
Date: Mon, 23 Aug 2004 3:15:55
Subject: Re: Ant Boy
From: Zach <zach@aol14.com>
To: Kate <kate@yahoo.com>

I didn't know you wanted to be vice president. I thought you hated politics. You can be my vice president only if YOU tell me the TRUTH. Did you write "Ant Boy" or not?

41

Re: Ant Boy

Date: Mon, 23 Aug 2004 3:44:22
Subject: Re: Ant Boy
From: Kate <kate@yahoo.com>
To: Zach <zach@aol14.com>

Yes, I would like to be class vice president, thank you. If you look back closely at these e-mails, you will see that I never actually denied that I wrote "Ant Boy." Anyway, I think Ant Boy is a cute name! That's why I wrote it! You certainly stand out from the other candidates now, Zach. On to victory!

1. **How is this story told?**

   Ⓐ by telephone   Ⓒ by postcards

   Ⓑ by e-mail   Ⓓ by posters

2. **When does the story take place?**

   _____

   _____

3. **What is Zach's problem?**

   Ⓐ He has lost the election for class president.

   Ⓑ He wants to run for vice president of the class.

   Ⓒ He doesn't know for sure who wrote on his election poster.

   Ⓓ He doesn't have any friends in school.

4. **What is the relationship between Kate and Zach?**

   Ⓐ sister and brother   Ⓒ enemies

   Ⓑ best friends   Ⓓ mother and son

5. **What is the mood of this story?**

   Ⓐ sad   Ⓒ playful

   Ⓑ serious   Ⓓ frightening

Name _____ Date _____

LeBron James Launches P.E. Program and a New Career
by Jesse Whitaker

Akron, Ohio—On September 8, NBA rookie LeBron James wowed the students of Akron's Margaret Park Elementary School. He visited the school to help start a new physical education program. James said that he wanted to help kids in Akron get into shape. He hopes students in his hometown have a chance to play sports.

In 2003, James became a professional basketball player in the NBA. He was drafted by the Cleveland Cavaliers as their first pick. Unlike many players who go to the NBA, James didn't go to college first. He went from high school to the pros at the age of 18. He was 6 feet 8 inches tall and weighed 240 pounds.

James was born in Akron, Ohio, on December 30, 1984. His mother was the most important person in his life growing up. By the time James entered high school, everyone in Akron knew he was a good basketball player. At St. Vincent–St. Mary High School, he became the star of the basketball team. He usually scored about 30 points per game. He led his team to the Division III State Championship. In his senior year, he was on the cover of *Sports Illustrated*!

Some people say that James will be the greatest basketball player ever. When he joined the Cavaliers, James signed a three-year contract worth almost $13 million. He got $4.02 million for his first year. He also signed advertising contracts worth close to $100 million.

No one has ever been paid the kind of money and attention that James has received before playing his first professional game. Many people will watch closely to see if James can live up to such high expectations.

---

1. What is this passage mostly about?

    Ⓐ a new physical education program

    Ⓑ basketball teams in Akron, Ohio

    Ⓒ the sports career of LeBron James

    Ⓓ how to become a player in the NBA

2. Write two details from the passage supporting the idea that James is already a huge star.

_____

_____

3. Another good title for this passage would be _____.

    Ⓐ LeBron James: Basketball Player

    Ⓑ The Cavaliers Draft James

    Ⓒ St. Vincent–St. Mary High School Graduates

    Ⓓ NBA Players

Passage 25   Main Idea and Supporting Details

Evelyn Trout:
A Remarkable Woman

On January 24, 2003, Evelyn "Bobbi" Trout passed away. She was 97. As one of the first women to fly airplanes, Trout did some amazing things. She held an international pilot's license that was signed by Orville Wright in 1929. Trout was also the last survivor of the 19 pilots who flew in the 1929 National Women's Air Derby, a race from California to Ohio. That was the race that made her famous.

Trout was born in Illinois in 1906—less than three years after the Wright brothers' first airplane flight. At 14, she began working at the family service station and became a good mechanic. (This skill served her well more than once when she began flying airplanes.) At the age of 16, Trout took her first plane ride from Rogers Airport in Los Angeles. From that moment on, she knew she wanted to be an aviator. She took her first flying lessons in 1928 and earned her solo pilot's license in four months. She also gained the nickname Bobbi when she had her hair "bobbed," or cut short. That was a popular style of the times.

Trout soon bought a biplane—a plane with two pairs of wings. She flew the biplane in many air shows around California. In late 1928 she accepted a job offer from a man named R.O. Bone. For $35 a week, she flew the new airplane he had just built. It was a monoplane called the Golden Eagle. A monoplane has one set of wings.

Trout set many aviator records. With the Golden Eagle she soon won an air race in Los Angeles. Then she set a new solo endurance record for women and made her first night landing. In 1929 Trout set the high-altitude record for light planes at 15,200 feet. The next year she won an air race in Burbank, California. In 1931, she and Edna May Cooper set a new world endurance record by flying nonstop for 122 hours, 50 minutes. Trout flew airplanes until 1984.

Trout received many awards and honors for her achievements. In 1933, she received the Aviation Gold Cross from the king of Romania. Only two other flyers had ever received this award before: Charles Lindbergh and Amelia Earhart. In 1976 she received the Outstanding Women's Award from the OX5 Aviation Pioneers.

In 1993, she was inducted into the Women in Aviation International Hall of Fame. In 1996, she received the Howard Hughes Memorial Award for her lifetime achievements in aviation. She was the first woman to receive this award.

In 1999 during an interview with the *Los Angeles Daily News*, Trout recalled the early days of flying. "People thought we were nuts," she said, describing how people reacted to her and other women pilots in the 1920s. But she certainly had a remarkable life.

1. What is this passage mostly about?

- Ⓐ why Evelyn Trout was called Bobbi
- Ⓑ the Powder Puff Derby
- Ⓒ Evelyn Trout's life as a pilot
- Ⓓ the Wright brothers

2. Which sentence best states the main idea of this passage?

- Ⓐ On January 24, 2003, Evelyn "Bobbi" Trout passed away in San Diego, California.
- Ⓑ As one of the first women to fly airplanes, Trout did some remarkable things.
- Ⓒ Trout held an international pilot's license that was signed by Orville Wright in 1929.
- Ⓓ Trout was also the last survivor of the 19 pilots who flew in the 1929 National Women's Air Derby, a race from California to Ohio.

3. Why was Trout's nickname "Bobbi?"

- Ⓐ She acted like a man.
- Ⓑ She had her hair cut short.
- Ⓒ She didn't like "Powder Puff."
- Ⓓ It was a popular name.

4. Write a detail from the passage to support the idea that Trout set many aviation records.

_____

_____

5. Write a detail from the passage to support the idea that Trout received many honors and awards for her achievements.

_____

_____

Answer Key

1. Frog Fest

1. C
2. She put a cotton ball with stuff on it that makes frogs sleep under the glass dome.
3. A
4. She let her frog go and ruined the class.
5. the sight of frogs

2. Being Yourself

1. A
2. D
3. Example: The author uses *The Wizard of Oz* characters as examples of people who think they could be special if they had certain qualities, but they learn that they already have those qualities and are already special.

3. Snip, Snip

1. B
2. A
3. C
4. D
5. Example: She cut one inch from the left leg, she cut two inches from the right leg, she cut two more inches from the right leg, and she cut the legs to make shorts.

4. On Top of the World

1. C
2. B
3. C
4. She was scared.
5. Example: She'll tell stories about her trip and show photos.

5. The Dog for You

1. D
2. dachshund, soft-coated wheaten terrier, Welsh terrier
3. dachshund, Doberman pinscher, German shepherd, Welsh terrier
4. D
5. dachshund, German shepherd, Old English sheepdog

Writing Prompt: Answers will vary.

6. The Snowball

1. D
2. Examples: It's warm in the middle of winter; there's fake snow falling; the government makes the snow.
3. A

7. River Raft Adventure!

1. B
2. A
3. C
4. B
5. Example: Fact: "I've been a rafting guide since 1988." Opinion: "You'll have a wonderful time!"

8. Let Everyone Play!

1. D
2. C
3. A
4. Example: Sports are fun.
5. B

Writing Prompt: Answers will vary.

9. School Uniforms? Think Again!

1. C
2. Answers should include any two of the following reasons: Uniforms make life easier for families. Parents do not have to decide what kind of clothes to buy for school. It's easier to get ready for school each day. Uniforms help children feel better about themselves. Uniforms make it easier for children of different backgrounds to make friends.
3. D
4. Answers will vary but should suggest that the writer does not like the idea of school uniforms. The writer says that uniforms "crush creativity" and suggests other problems with uniforms.
5. Answers will vary but should include a clear opinion in favor or against school uniforms and include at least one well-supported reason.

10. Meet a Snowboard Champ

1. Examples: It costs less to rent equipment than to buy it; if you try snowboarding and decide you don't like it, you won't waste a lot of money if you rented your equipment; you can try different kinds of equipment before choosing what to buy.
2. D
3. Example: It may be sunny when you snowboard. These things protect you from the sun; goggles and sunglasses can also help with the sun's glare.
4. It is attached to the snowboard and the snowboarder.
5. C

11. The Mysterious "Black Box"

1. B
2. C
3. A
4. They can find out problems about the airplane and make changes so the problems won't happen again.
5. Example: Questions about an accident could not be answered.

12. Ronnie's Restaurant Review

1. B
2. C
3. Examples: The strawberry shakes were too sweet and did not taste like real strawberries; the veggie burger is "so-so"; the salads are "ho-hum"; the Mexican burger had soggy chips and salsa that tasted store-bought.

13. Making a Sled Kite

1. A
2. Use the pattern as a guide for cutting out your kite shape. Put the paper under the pattern and trace around it. Then cut along the traced lines.
3. Decorate your kite.

4. Attach wooden sticks along each wing fold with packing tape.
5. Examples: Tie the string from the spool to the loop in the bridle; put the short stick through the hole in the spool of string.

14. It's a Wild and Wonderful Ride, But Is It Safe?

1. B
2. D
3. Examples: They can hear any new little sound or feel any new bump or jolt the coaster makes; several times a week they ride each coaster in the park to check for anything that seems different or concerns them; if they notice anything, however small, they let the people who repair the coaster know.

15. Isabel Leaves a Trail of Destruction

1. B
2. Example: Isabel was a huge storm and flying through it would be too dangerous.
3. Example: Yes. The article says people are leaving North Carolina because it's hurricane country.

16. Stick-to-it-ive Brian

1. D
2. A
3. C
4. A
5. At the shopping mall and in Brian's room
Writing Prompt: Answers will vary.

17. Blue Jeans

1. D
2. B
3. In the 1850s they cost 22 cents but today some jeans can cost more than $100.
4. Then: miners and railroad men; today: all kinds of people including toddlers, teens, and seniors

5. Then: for work; now: for work but also for other occasions such as play, parties and school

18. Welcome to Moviefans.com!

1. A
2. Example: Yes, because a grip would *grip*, or handle equipment.
3. It wouldn't be good to show the microphone in the movie with actors.
4. Example: Yes, because someone on the swing gang builds or tears down sets and would be swinging hammers and other tools.
5. Answers will vary.

19. Come Meet Our New Pals—The Sloth Bears

1. D
2. A
3. Examples: Sloth bears can hang in trees; they have long, shaggy fur; they have large, floppy ears; they have long pointed noses; their stomachs have almost no fur; they eat mostly termites; they have only 40 adult teeth; they do not have a long winter's sleep; mother sloth bears carry their cubs on their backs; they can close their nostrils at will.

20. Spiders

1. C
2. C
3. Fact: No two webs are ever the same; opinion: This is really amazing.

21. Book Review: *Darkness over Denmark*

1. B
2. Danes learned of the Germans' plans and fought back to save Danish Jews.
3. It has dramatic tales of rescue.

22. Egg Rolls

1. Get all the ingredients ready.
2. A
3. Warm with a dipping sauce

23. Vote for Zach and . . .

1. B
2. Monday, August 23, between 10:44 AM and 3:45 PM
3. C
4. B
5. C

24. LeBron James Launches P.E. Program and a New Career

1. C
2. Examples: He was on the cover of *Sports Illustrated*; he signed a three-year contract worth almost $13 million; he signed advertising contracts worth nearly $100 million.
3. A

25. Evelyn Trout: A Remarkable Woman

1. C
2. B
3. B
4. Examples: She set a solo endurance record for women; she set the high-altitude record in 1929; she set a world endurance record in 1931.
5. Examples: She received the Aviation Gold Cross, the Outstanding Women's Award, the Howard Hughes Memorial Award, and was inducted into the Women in Aviation International Hall of Fame.